NORRIE EXPLORES...

CHICAGO

Help Norrie to solve the clues on a fascinating adventure!

World Book, Inc.
180 North LaSalle Street
Suite 900
Chicago, Illinois 60601
USA

For information about other World Book publications, visit our website at www.worldbook.com or call 1-800-WORLDBK (967-5325). For information about sales to schools and libraries, call 1-800-975-3250 (United States), or 1-800-837-5365 (Canada).

Library of Congress Cataloging-in-Publication Data for this volume has been applied for.

Norrie Explores ...
ISBN: 978-0-7166-5303-5 (set, hc.)

Norrie Explores ... Chicago
ISBN: 978-0-7166-5307-3 (hc.)
ISBN: 978-0-7166-5327-1 (pf.)

Also available as:
ISBN: 978-0-7166-5317-2 (e-book)

Staff

Executive Committee
President: Geoff Broderick
Vice President, Editorial: Tom Evans
Vice President, Finance: Donald D. Keller
Vice President, International: Eddy Kisman
Vice President, Technology: Jason Dole
Director, Human Resources: Bev Ecker

Editorial
Senior Editor/Indexer: Shawn Brennan
Editor/Researcher: Lynn Durbin
Content Creator: Jenna Neely
Curriculum Designer: Caroline Davidson
Project Coordinator: Kaile Kilner
Proofreader: Nathalie Strassheim

Graphics and Design
Senior Visual Communications Designer: Melanie Bender
Senior Media Editor: Rosalia Bledsoe

Acknowledgments

Writer: Madeline King
Illustrator: Mike Garton, The Bright Agency
Designer: Francis Lea

Cover: Norrie artwork by Mike Garton, The Bright Agency; © beboy/Shutterstock

4-7 © Shutterstock
8-9 © Bruce Leighty, Alamy Images; © Museum of Science and Industry - Chicago
10-11 © Thomas Barrat, Shutterstock; © Martin Baumgaertner, Field Museum; © Man Hurt/Shutterstock; © Vostapenko/Shutterstock
12-13 © Hendrickson Photography/Shutterstock; © Brenna Hernandez, Shedd Aquarium; © Robert Sarnowski, Shutterstock
14-15 © Adler Planetarium; © Jeremy Graham, Alamy Images
16-17 © Claude Gariepy, Shutterstock; © f11photo/Shutterstock; *A Sunday Afternoon on the Island of La Grande Jatte* (1884-1886), oil on canvas by Georges Seurat; Art Institute of Chicago
18-19 © MaxyM/Shutterstock; *A Sunday Afternoon on the Island of La Grande Jatte* (1884-1886), oil on canvas by Georges Seurat; Art Institute of Chicago; © EmmePi Images/Alamy Images; WORLD BOOK photo by Tom Evans
20-21 © Photo Spirit/Shutterstock; © James Byard, Alamy Images; © Sergii Figurnyi, Shutterstock
22-23 © Evgenia Parajanian, Shutterstock; © Everett Collection/Alamy Images
24-25 Chicago History Museum; © Bruce Leighty, Alamy Images; © EQRoy/Shutterstock
26-27 © Shutterstock
28-29 © Leonid Andronov, Shutterstock; © Pictorial Press/Alamy Images
30-31 © Gregory Holmgren, Alamy Images; © Dan Peterman
32-33 © Pgiam/iStock; © Page Light Studios/Shutterstock; © Thomas Barrat, Shutterstock
34-35 © Shutterstock
36-37 © Alisafarov/Shutterstock; © Wirestock Creators/Shutterstock; © Michael Heimlich, Shutterstock; © Felix Choo, Alamy Images; © Julia G. Reed, Shutterstock; © Westend61 GmbH/Alamy Images
38-39 © Hemis/Alamy Images; Library of Congress
40-41 © John Lupu, Shutterstock; © Cal Sport Media/Alamy Images; © UPI/Alamy Images; © Zuma Press/Alamy Images
42-43 © Matt Dirksen, Getty Images; © Bruce Leighty, Alamy Images
46-47 © Henryk Sadura, Shutterstock; © Ian Dagnall, Alamy Images; © CKP1001/Shutterstock; © Panoramic Images/Alamy Images; © Supitcha McAdam, Shutterstock; © Jerry Lai, Alamy Images
48-49 © Shutterstock; © Kim Karpeles, Alamy Images
50-51 © Roy Johnson, Alamy Stock Photo; © Shutterstock

Contents

Welcome to Chicago!

Hi, my name is Norrie. I'm a type of bird called a puffin. I love to travel the world. I hope you will come with me.

In this book, we will visit Chicago, which is the third largest city in the United States. Only New York City and Los Angeles, in California, have more people than Chicago.

My friend Ernie, who is a northern cardinal, lives in Chicago and is a huge baseball fan. Chicago is known for its two Major League Baseball (MLB) teams. The rivalry, or competition, between them is strong! In Chicago, you're either a Cubs fan or a White Sox fan. Which team should I support?

Ernie says that in order for me to pick a team, I need to get to know Chicago better. He has put together a treasure hunt for me. If I solve the clues, Ernie will take me to a baseball game. The clues will be photos, words, or objects. As I follow the clues, I will get to see Chicago.

Hyde Park

I solved my first clue! It's a stained glass window from Robie House in Hyde Park!

Let's take a walk through this neighborhood to see some of Chicago's spectacular architecture. This is the neighborhood of the world-famous University of Chicago. There are chapels and libraries in the fancy Gothic style. But there are also modern laboratories and arts centers.

Now we are at the Robie House. I hope you like long rectangles, because this home has thousands of them! Look for rectangles and other shapes in the bricks, the windows, the furniture, and the lamps. Who came up with this unusual design? One of Chicago's most famous architects, Frank Lloyd Wright. He wanted to design a home that matched the wide plains found in this part of the country. He called the design "prairie style."

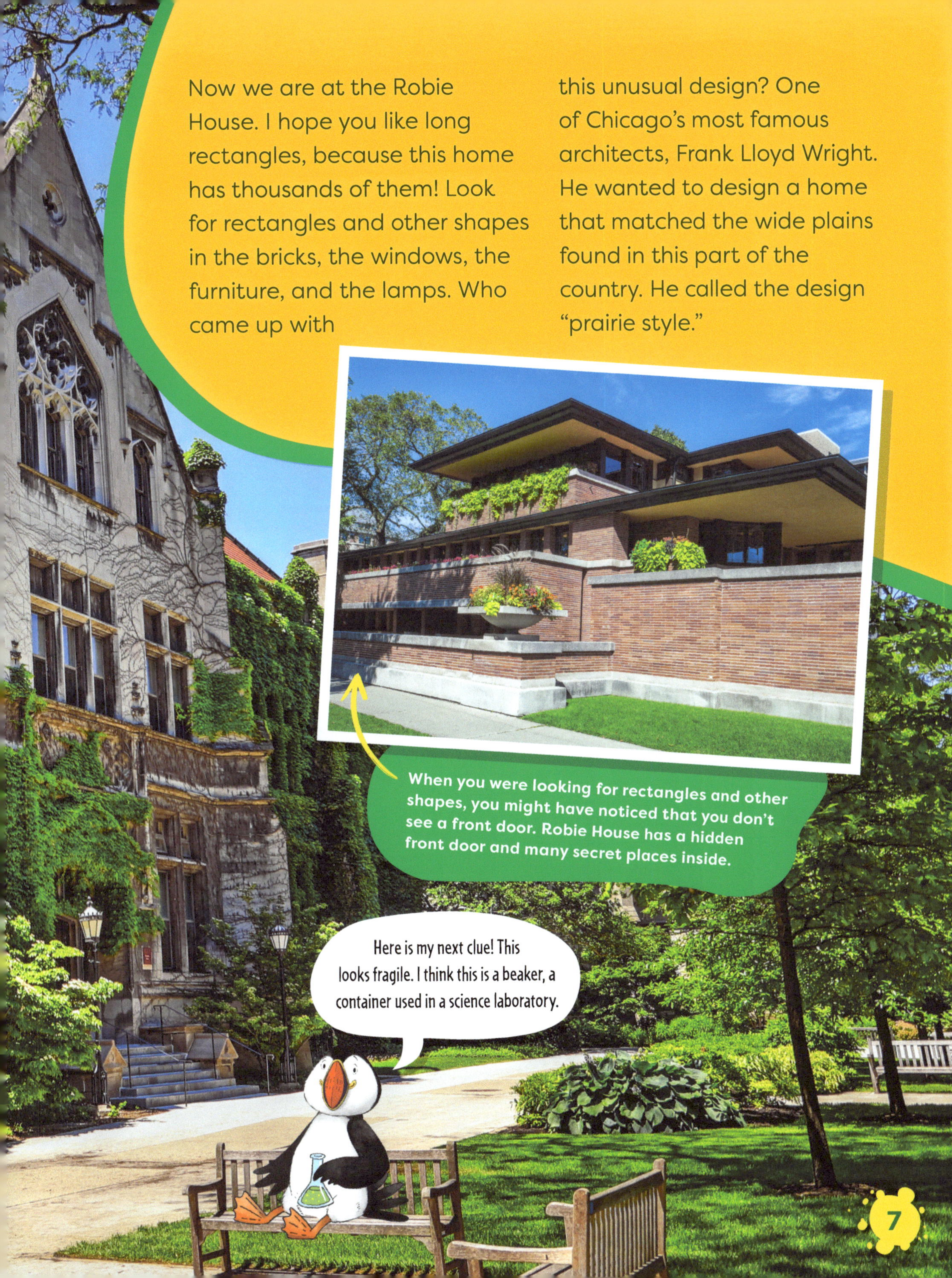

When you were looking for rectangles and other shapes, you might have noticed that you don't see a front door. Robie House has a hidden front door and many secret places inside.

Museum of Science and Industry

I am on a roll – I solved my second clue! Now we are at the Museum of Science and Industry.

This is one of my favorite museums. It is the largest and most popular science and technology museum in the United States. Opened in 1933, it is designed to further public understanding of science and the use of science in industry by presenting enlightening and entertaining exhibits, educational programs, and other activities. The museum has lots of interactive exhibits – things for us to do and try. At the Science Storms exhibit, we can control a giant tornado spinning in the middle of the room.

This grand building was built as part of the "White City," an attraction of the 1893 Columbian Exposition. The exposition was a huge celebration called a world's fair. It gave Chicago a chance to show off how well it had recovered from the Great Fire. In October 1871, the Great Chicago Fire swept through downtown. Most of the city was made of wood and easily burned.
The museum has over 400,000 square feet (37,000 square meters) of floor space. I'm glad I can fly – that would be a lot of ground to cover on foot!"
Now it's time for my third clue. This looks like a dinosaur bone. I thought dinosaurs disappeared nearly 66 million years ago ...

Field Museum

I have to say hi to my friend, Sue. Sue is the largest nearly complete skeleton of *Tyrannosaurus rex* – a type of dinosaur – ever discovered. Sue measures 42 feet (13 meters) in length.

The Field Museum is one of the world's largest natural history museums. The museum's collections include more than 30 million items, including both artifacts (things made by people) and natural objects.

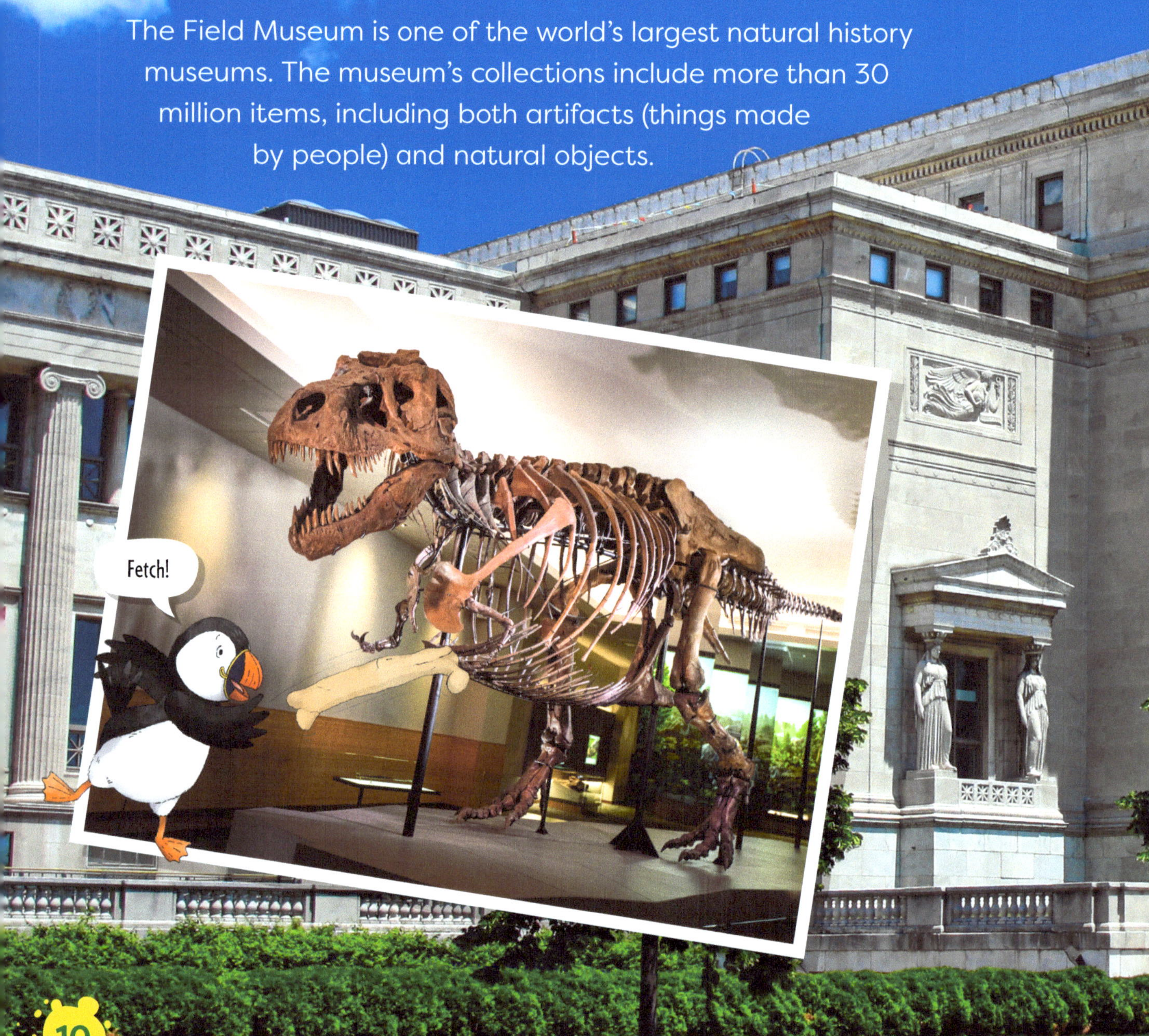

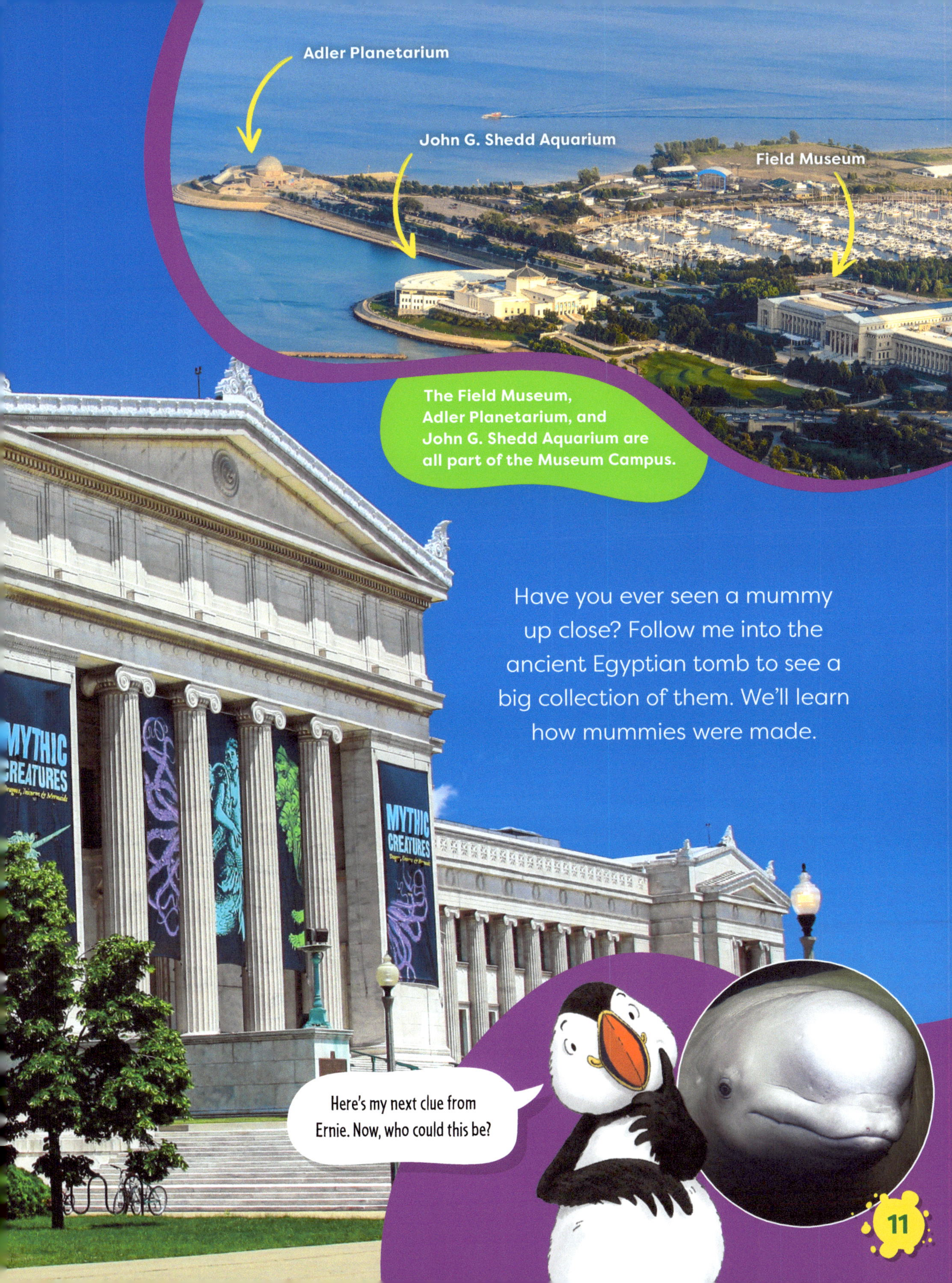

Have you ever seen a mummy up close? Follow me into the ancient Egyptian tomb to see a big collection of them. We'll learn how mummies were made.

John G. Shedd Aquarium

Next on the Museum Campus we'll visit the John G. Shedd Aquarium, on the Lake Michigan shore.

There, we can see fish and other aquatic creatures from around the world. At the Shedd you can see the largest fish in Lake Michigan, the lake sturgeon. It can grow as long as 8 feet (2.4 meters). That's the distance from your bedroom floor to the ceiling. We'll also meet turtles, coral reef fish, beluga whales, and playful otters.

AQUARIUM
John G. Shedd Aquarium
Chicago is on the shores of Lake Michigan. Lake Michigan is the third largest of the Great Lakes, a group of five lakes in the United States and Canada. The other lakes are Superior, Huron, Erie, and Ontario.
Exit only
An astronaut helmet? Where is this going to take me?

Adler Planetarium

Our last stop on the Museum Campus is the Adler Planetarium. It's a great place to learn about outer space.

Do you ever lie on your back and look at the stars? In the planetarium's sky theater, we can sit back in total darkness and see pictures so realistic that it feels like we're flying between galaxies.

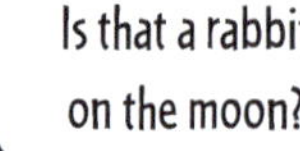

The Adler Planetarium, the first planetarium in the western hemisphere, opened to the public in 1930.
Before we go, let's check out the Gemini 12 spacecraft. Astronauts rode it into orbit around Earth. If the weather is just right, we can also look at the sun through the Doane Observatory telescope.
What's this next clue? A bottle of water! What's that about?

Buckingham Fountain

There's plenty of water here! We are at Buckingham Fountain. It is a lovely summer attraction.

The fountain operates daily from mid-April to mid-October. It contains about 1 ½ million gallons (5.7 million liters) of water and shoots its central spout about 150 feet (45 meters) in the air. From Buckingham Fountain, the views include Lake Michigan to the east and downtown skyscrapers to the west and north. You can see some of them in this picture!

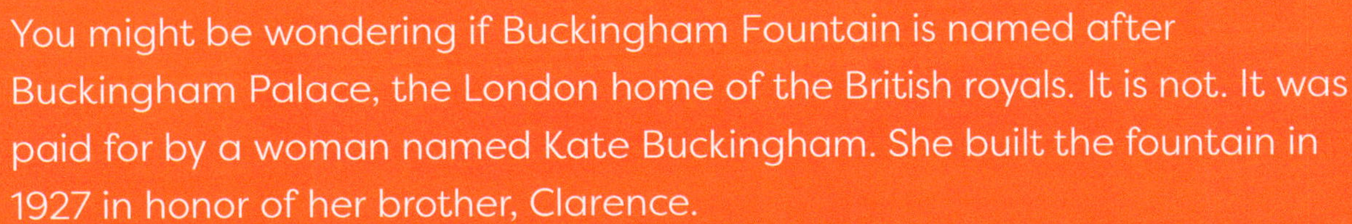

You might be wondering if Buckingham Fountain is named after Buckingham Palace, the London home of the British royals. It is not. It was paid for by a woman named Kate Buckingham. She built the fountain in 1927 in honor of her brother, Clarence.

The fountain is in Grant Park, named after former United States President Ulysses S. Grant. People come here to walk, go jogging, have a picnic, or take a boat ride on the lake. What should I do first?

At night, the fountain is lit by a dazzling display of colored lights. It is one of the world's largest lighted fountains.

The fountain has four seahorses. Each seahorse represents one state that borders Lake Michigan. The states are Illinois, Indiana, Michigan, and Wisconsin.

Hey, here's my next clue. What a beautiful painting!

Art Institute of Chicago

The heart of downtown Chicago is called the Loop. That's where we'll find the Art Institute, a giant art museum. Huge statues of lions guard the entrance.

Inside the museum, you can see many famous paintings. One of the most famous is *A Sunday Afternoon on the Island of La Grande Jatte* by the French artist Georges Seurat. (You say that name zhawrzh suh RAH.) This masterpiece was our clue! This huge painting shows a park scene.

If you look closely, you will see the picture is made up of thousands of tiny hand-painted dots. It took two years to paint.

There are more than just paintings at the Art Institute. Don't forget to check out their collection of arms and armor from medieval and Renaissance times (the 400's to the 1500's). You'll see swords, armor, and other weapons used by knights, soldiers, and hunters. There are even two life-sized warriors on horseback.

Part of the museum overlooks Millennium Park.

Millennium Park

The mirror takes us to our next destination: Millennium Park. This park is home to a very famous sculpture called *The Bean*.

This huge piece of public art is called The Bean because ... it is shaped like a bean! The sculpture's real name is *Cloud Gate*. Its shiny metal surface reflects the Chicago skyline and whatever silly faces we make when we stand close to it.

We can also see the Lurie Garden. What a delightful green place! Butterflies flap and honey bees buzz among the prairie plants. Millennium Park is a popular park for picnics, outdoor concerts, garden walks, and splashing in fountains.
Water sprays from the towers, looking like it's being spit from the mouths of the faces. It looks funny, and it feels cool on a hot day!
Two tall towers stand in the park's Crown Fountain. The towers are covered in clear glass bricks. The bricks are lit from within by special lights called LED's. The LED's glow in various colors. Some of them shine giant pictures of the faces of Chicagoans.
This might be my favorite clue yet - an ice cream cone! I know this place is going to be good.

Navy Pier

The delicious ice cream cone has led us to Navy Pier. Wow, look at that huge Ferris wheel. Let's ride it!

This Ferris wheel has cars that close completely, so we can ride it even in winter. As we go up, check out the great views of the skyline. You can also see the rest of the pier stretching into Lake Michigan.

Navy Pier didn't always have rides, theaters, restaurants, and boat cruises. It was built in 1916. Then, it was used by passenger ships and cargo ships that traveled the lake. Navy Pier doesn't handle cargo ships today. But, freighters and barges still pass through Chicago. They carry such things as steel, iron ore, and wheat.

The city's rivers link the Great Lakes and the Mississippi River. Boats can get from here to the Atlantic Ocean. The Port of Chicago is one of the country's busiest.

Skyscrapers

Now I see why we need binoculars. We're visiting famous Chicago skyscrapers. When we're in the tall skyscrapers, we can use the binoculars to see the city!

The skyscraper was invented in Chicago. The Great Chicago Fire in 1871 destroyed much of downtown. But it wasn't long before architects and engineers drew up plans for new buildings. They designed buildings with frames of steel covered in stone. No wood this time. They also planned buildings to rise up instead of spread out.

Good thing I'm not afraid of heights. Hmmm, are there any birds afraid of heights ... ?

An architect named William Le Baron Jenney designed the Home Insurance Building in the early 1880's. It rose 10 stories into the sky. You might not think that's very tall. But back then, it was amazing. The building was torn down in 1931. But the steel frame design that made it famous is still used around the world today.

875 N. Michigan Ave.
1,128 ft. (344 m.) tall
100 floors

Fun fact:
The building's frame is on the outside instead of the inside. See the X-shaped braces?

Willis Tower
1,450 ft. (442 m.) tall
110 floors

Fun fact:
The elevators travel at 1,600 feet (488 meters) per minute.

Chicago River

While I am not taking a dip in beautiful Lake Michigan, I am at another body of water in Chicago: the Chicago River. The river runs through the heart of the city.

Native Americans were the first people to live in this area. Wild onions used to grow along the riverbanks. The name Chicago comes from a Native American word for wild onions.

Native Americans called the Potawatomi traveled on the river hundreds of years ago. They paddled their canoes on the river to meet other nearby Native Americans. The people would trade with one another. In 1803, the U.S. government built Fort Dearborn, at the place where Michigan Avenue now crosses the river. Traders and farmers settled around it. The settlement grew to become the city.

Bridges can rise up along the Chicago River, allowing tall sailboats to pass underneath. The bridges are raised in the spring to allow boats to enter Lake Michigan. In the fall, they are raised so that boats can return to storage.

Every March, crowds gather at the river when the city dyes its waters green for St. Patrick's Day, a day that honors the patron saint of Ireland. Chicago has a large number of people of Irish descent.
Oh my! The next clue is a piece of limestone. Where is that taking me?

Water Tower

I know! The Water Tower is made of limestone.

This important landmark is located on Michigan Avenue. Fancy, modern buildings line this part of the avenue, called the "Magnificent Mile." But the historic Water Tower looks different – it looks like a tower in a fairy tale.

The Water Tower and the pumping station were built in 1869. Inside them is part of the pipe system that pumped the city's water from Lake Michigan. One of the pipes was really tall. The water tower was built around it. In October 1871, the Great Chicago Fire swept through downtown. Most of the city was made of wood and easily burned. The water tower and pumping station are made out of limestone. They were two of the few downtown buildings that survived!

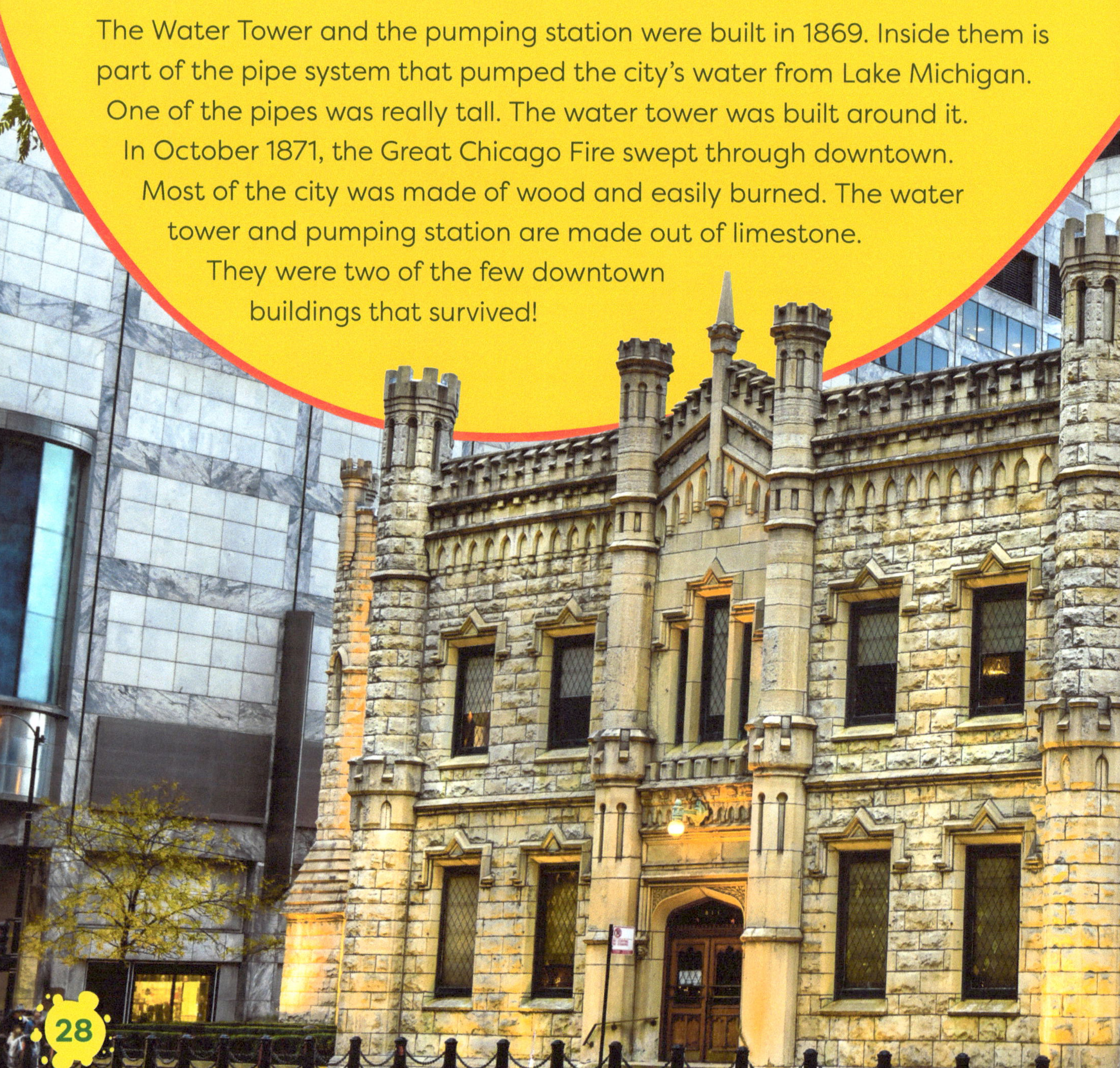

Chicago's flag has two blue stripes and four red stars. Each star stands for an important event in the city's history. One star is for the Great Chicago Fire, one is for Fort Dearborn, and two are for the city's world fairs.
The Great Chicago Fire left nearly one-third of the city's population homeless.
My next clue is very colorful. I hope it's meant for protection from the sun–not rain!

Lakefront Beaches

On hot summer days, I love feeling the sand between my webbed feet!

Chicago has lots of sandy beaches along Lake Michigan. They are connected by the Lakefront Trail. I like to swim and play volleyball at Oak Street Beach and North Avenue Beach. The North Avenue Beach House is shaped like a steamboat. They sell ice cream there. Yum!

Many Chicago beaches used to be really narrow until the 1920's. Then the city added to the shoreline, dumping sand along the lake. Barges hauled the sand from the Indiana Dunes – big hills of sand – across the lake. The city has also built breakwater barriers. These offshore walls of rock and other material protect the shoreline from being washed away by waves.

Shipwrecked! Look for the wreck of the ship *Silver Spray.* It pokes out of Lake Michigan just off 49th Street Beach. This wooden steamship ran aground in 1914. Several ships have sunk along the Chicago shore. Lake Michigan can be fierce. Winds can create waves as high as a two-story house!

Lakefront Trail

Oh! This is nice. I had worried we were going to visit a famous treadmill in Chicago. This trail is gorgeous! I will be happy here.

You might have noticed lots of bicycles and runners around the lakefront parks and the Museum Campus. Many people bike or run along the Lakefront Trail, a paved pathway along the shore of Lake Michigan. It runs way up to the North Side, way past Navy Pier, and way south, past the Museum of Science and Industry. It stretches 18.5 miles (30 kilometers)!

Look over one shoulder, and you will see parks and tall buildings. Look the other way for sandy beaches along Lake Michigan. Wow! The lake is so huge that we can't see the other side. It seems like we're next to the ocean! That makes me think of home ...

Are we running the entire way?

You can find a variety of attractions along the trail

- 26 beaches
- 13 neighborhoods
- 7 boat harbors
- 1 zoo

Check out the Riverwalk for a different shoreline stroll. This path runs next to the Chicago River, on its south bank. We'll go underneath some of the city's famous lifting bridges.

Chicago Eats

Are you hungry? Chicago has just about any kind of food. But some foods are unique to Chicago. Perhaps the city's most famous food is its deep-dish pizza.

Chicago-style pizza is probably thicker and cheesier than you're used to. It may measure 2 inches (5 centimeters) thick! The crust curves up the sides and holds heaps of toppings. I am thankful for whoever dreamed this up. I like that the thick crust holds many toppings. The toppings are upside down compared with other pizzas. My favorite toppings are pepperoni, mushrooms, and spinach. Chunky tomato sauce sits on the top, with cheese underneath.

Are you a messy eater? You will be when you try an Italian beef sandwich. Extra meat will fall out onto the table. Delicious beef juice will drip onto your shirt! Even puffins need extra napkins. I wonder if Italian beef would be good on a slice of famous Chicago deep-dish pizza.

This sandwich was created in Chicago's Little Italy neighborhood, on the west side of Chicago, during the Great Depression (economic hard times in the 1930's). The people there sliced beef really thin and served it on thick slices of fresh bread.

Lincoln Park Zoo

It's time to visit my favorite place in any city – the zoo! Today, we're visiting the Lincoln Park Zoo.

We'll visit farm animals from the U.S. Midwest, African animals, and some of my friends from the Arctic. The zoo is free to visit. It opened in 1868. It is one of America's oldest zoos. I really feel at home here. There's a lion house. That's how I knew where we were supposed to come. I wonder if the lions ever visit their friends at the Art Institute of Chicago ...

There are also chimpanzees. What are the chimpanzees doing? The chimps are eating from a termite mound.

It might seem strange that lions and chimpanzees can live near skyscrapers. The zookeepers work hard to create comfortable homes for them.

Workers at the zoo also study wildlife that lives in the city – bats, chipmunks, deer, and coyotes, to name a few.

I wonder if I'll find any of these animal friends on my journey throughout Chicago. Maybe they like Italian beef sandwiches – I know I do!

The zoo is located in a huge park called Lincoln Park, named after Abraham Lincoln. He lived most of his life in Illinois, before becoming president of the United States in 1861. You can see this statue of him in the park.
What's that wonderful sound? I think it's coming from my next clue: a saxophone. I'm not very musically inclined, but maybe I am in Chicago!

Blues

I'm smart – I knew the saxophone would lead us somewhere musical.

What's your favorite kind of music? Many Chicagoans love the blues. Blues is a kind of music started by African Americans. It has its roots in songs sung by people who were enslaved and workers in farm fields. Blues songs are often about feeling blue, or sad.

In the 1900's, many African Americans from the South moved north to Chicago. They were looking for jobs in the city's factories. Musicians brought harmonicas, guitars, and the blues with them. There were also electric guitars, which created a style known as the Chicago blues. Since then, Chicago has been a popular place to

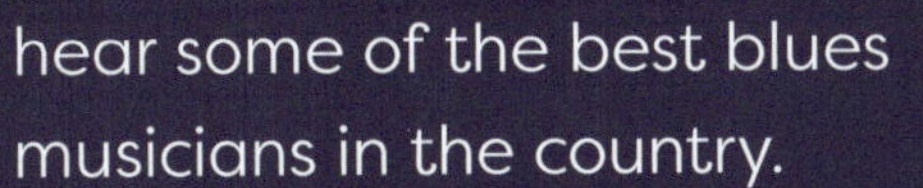

hear some of the best blues musicians in the country.

Blues influenced many other kinds of music. The blues contributed greatly to the development of jazz. In addition, a lot of rhythm and blues (R&B), soul, rock and roll, and hard rock music shows the influence of the blues.

The Great Migration: From 1915 to 1970, more than 6 million African Americans moved from the rural South to such northern cities as New York City, Detroit, and Chicago.

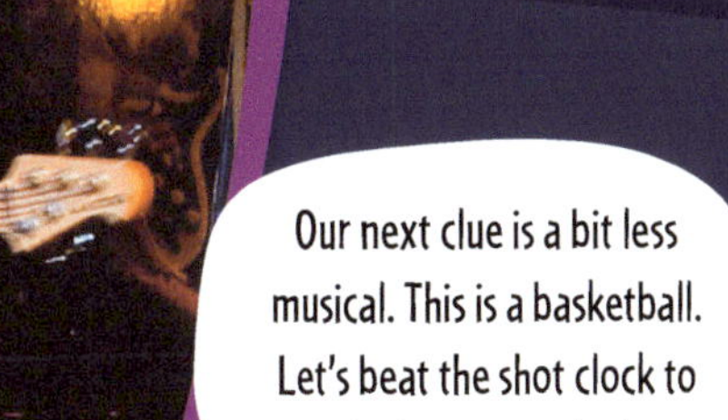

Sports Town

Chicago is one of the world's greatest sports towns.

That's why I'm especially excited to watch a baseball game! Many of Chicago's professional teams have a long history, with several championships. But it is the loyalty of the fans that is the most remarkable. Walk anywhere in Chicago, and you'll see someone proudly wearing a local team jersey or cap.

The Bears – Football
Home field: Soldier Field. In the future, they plan to play in the Chicago suburb of Arlington Heights.
Gameday traditions: Before the game, fans grill hot dogs and sausages and throw footballs around in the parking lot. It's called a tailgate party!

The Bulls – Basketball

Home court: United Center

Gameday traditions: Before the game, the stadium goes dark. A loud theme song plays, and a light show flashes as the Bulls are introduced. The crowd goes wild!

The Blackhawks – Hockey

Home ice: United Center

Gameday traditions: Before the puck is dropped, fans sing the national anthem at the top of their lungs. It's so loud you can't even hear the lead singer at the microphone.

Chicago Fire – Soccer

Home field: Soldier Field

Gameday traditions: You might feel some of the excitement of Latin America at a Chicago Fire soccer game. Fans cheer on the team with songs and chants, sometimes in Spanish. *Vamos* means let's go!

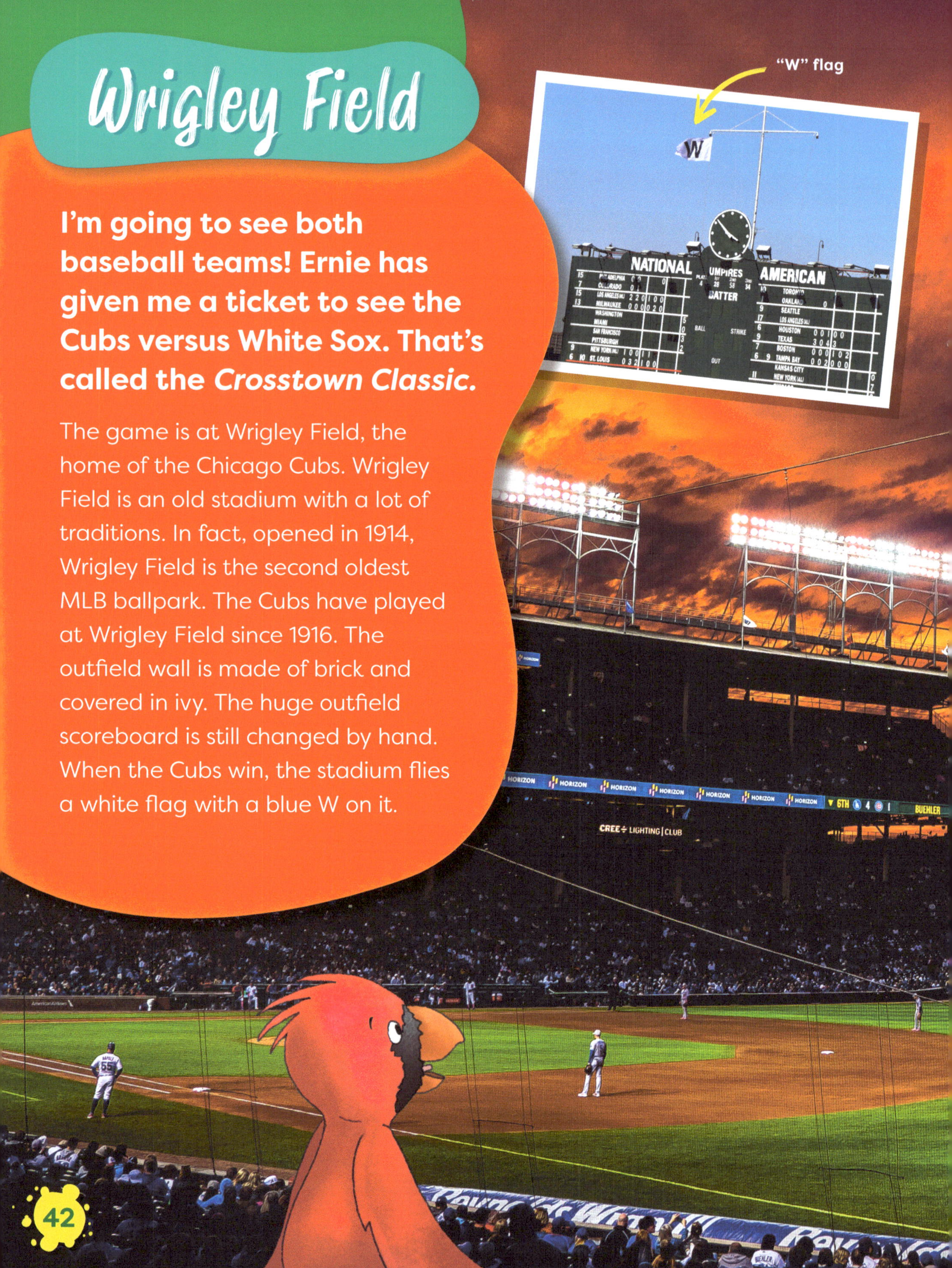

Wrigley Field

I'm going to see both baseball teams! Ernie has given me a ticket to see the Cubs versus White Sox. That's called the *Crosstown Classic.*

The game is at Wrigley Field, the home of the Chicago Cubs. Wrigley Field is an old stadium with a lot of traditions. In fact, opened in 1914, Wrigley Field is the second oldest MLB ballpark. The Cubs have played at Wrigley Field since 1916. The outfield wall is made of brick and covered in ivy. The huge outfield scoreboard is still changed by hand. When the Cubs win, the stadium flies a white flag with a blue W on it.

The Chicago White Sox play in a home stadium called Guaranteed Rate Field. It's on the south side of Chicago. Perhaps on my next trip to the city, I will visit there.

I had a wonderful time in Chicago! I loved learning more about the city and its history. I'm really excited to watch the baseball game. I wonder who will win today? I think I'll support both Chicago teams!

CHICAGO
- MAP -

Chicago River

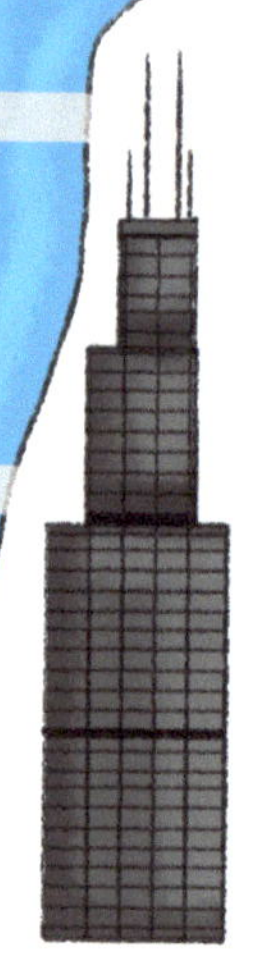

875 N. Michigan Avenue
Navy Pier
Cloud Gate
Lake Michigan
Art Institute of Chicago
Buckingham Fountain
John G. Shedd Aquarium
Adler Planetarium
Field Museum

A Day in Chicago

Looking for hands-on STEM experiences? Don't worry, the Museum of Science and Industry isn't too far away!

Welcome to the Windy City! Let's begin our day at the Museum Campus. What will you learn?

Make your way to the Loop and take a guided tour of Chicago's architecture and history as you cruise down the Chicago River.

After all that learning you must be hungry! Grab some lunch at a local vendor or restaurant. Will you try a Chicago-style hot dog?

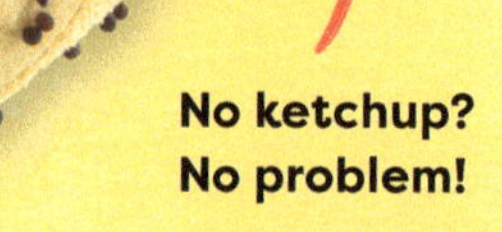

No ketchup? No problem!

Locals love summer in the city. Let's go join in the fun at one of Chicago's lakefront beaches.

From swimming in Lake Michigan, to building a sand castle or playing beach volleyball, what will you choose first?

Look at all that ooey gooey cheese!

It's dinnertime! Fill up on some of Chicago's famous deep-dish pizza.

Remember to take a spin on the Ferris wheel.

Head over to Navy Pier for some evening entertainment. Enjoy shopping, rides, games, live music, and more. If you're lucky, you may even catch the fireworks!

Where Am I?

Destination 1

This site opened in 1868 and is one of the oldest of its kind in America.

This location is named after a former United States president who was raised in Illinois.

Visitors can enjoy exhibits from the Midwest, Africa, Antarctica, and more on a fun trip to this free destination.

Destination 2

At this destination, people can enjoy a water display, even at night, when it is lit up in bright colors.

This site is located in Grant Park and has great views of downtown Chicago and Lake Michigan.

Although its name sounds like a famous London Palace, this memorial was actually named by the woman who paid for it in her brother's honor.

Destination 3

This historic destination can be found on the "Magnificent Mile," part of Michigan Avenue in downtown Chicago.

Unlike most of the city, these buildings survived the Great Chicago Fire of 1871 because they were made of limestone.

Built in 1869, these buildings helped pump water from Lake Michigan for use in the city.

Destination 4

Frank Lloyd Wright designed one of this neighborhood's most famous buildings, the Robie House.

Visitors can admire the Gothic-style architecture of chapels, libraries, and more while also enjoying the more modern laboratories or arts centers located here.

The world-famous University of Chicago is located in this neighborhood.

Destination 5

The green space, butterflies, and honey bees at Lurie Garden, located here, are a nice break from the bustling city.

During the warmer months, kids play and laugh at the funny faces on the tall towers at Crown Fountain.

It may be called Cloud Gate, but most know this destination's iconic sculpture as The Bean.

Destination 6

This destination is known for its brick outfield wall that is covered in ivy.

Unlike many other stadiums across the United States, this location's scoreboard is still changed manually, or by hand.

Home of the Chicago Cubs, this is the second oldest ballpark in Major League Baseball.

Answers on page 55

Photos from Chicago

Navy Pier

Field Museum

Buckingham Fountain

Art Institute of Chicago

Millennium Park

Michigan Avenue

Oak Street Beach

Engage Your Reader

Activate background knowledge, set the purpose for reading, and monitor comprehension with this tried-and-true reading strategy!

Work with your reader(s) to create a KWL chart. Take some time to discuss what students already KNOW about Chicago as well as what they WONDER about the city. You will revisit what they LEARNED after reading the book.

KNOW	WONDER	LEARNED

1. Have readers preview the structure of this text by flipping through the pages. Page 5 describes how clues are included for Norrie's next destinations.
2. Set the tone for reading: *As you read, think about all the different places in Chicago and how history, culture, and people have shaped them into what they are today.*
3. After reading each section, revisit the KWL chart. Brainstorm what readers LEARNED from this section and add it to the chart. Your reader can add other wonderings they may have had, too!

Consider these questions to guide the brainstorming process:

- Why is location important to places, history, and culture?
- What patterns do you notice in the placement of things around the city of Chicago?
- What makes Chicago unique?

Use these comprehension questions to help your reader(s) check their understanding as they navigate the text.

p. 6-7 What famous university can be found in Hyde Park?

Who was Frank Lloyd Wright?

p. 8-9 Why might the massive Museum of Science and Industry have many interactive exhibits?

p. 10-11 What type of museum is the Field Museum?

Who is Sue?

p. 12-13 What aquatic animals can be found at the John G. Shedd Aquarium?

p. 14-15 What can visitors do at Adler Planetarium?

p. 16-17 What do the four seahorses on Buckingham Fountain represent?

p. 18-19 Where is the Art Institute of Chicago located?

p. 20-21 What would you enjoy doing in Millennium Park?

p. 22-23 When and where was the Ferris wheel invented?

p. 24-25 How did architects and engineers change downtown Chicago after the Great Fire in 1871?

p. 26-27 From where did the city of Chicago get its name?

p. 28-29 How did the historic Water Tower survive the Great Chicago Fire?

p. 30-31 What would you most enjoy about a trip to one of Chicago's many lakefront beaches?

p. 32-33 How long is Chicago's Lakefront Trail, and where does it run?

p. 34-35 Would you rather eat a slice of Chicago's famous deep-dish pizza or a juicy Italian beef sandwich? Why?

p. 36-37 When did the Lincoln Park Zoo open, and who is it named after?

p. 38-39 How did blues music become popular in Chicago?

p. 40-41 Which Chicago sports teams and arenas interest you? Why?

p. 42-43 What is special about the outfield scoreboard at Wrigley Field?

Extend Through Writing

Norrie just took you on a tour of Chicago, United States of America! Based on the places highlighted in this book, where would you like to visit in Chicago?

Your written response should include:

- An introduction, including a general statement about Chicago
- At least three places you would like to visit and at least three reasons why these places interest you
- A conclusion in which you briefly restate your interest in these three famous Chicago destinations

Copy this graphic organizer onto another sheet of paper or visit **www.worldbook.com/resources** to download and print a copy. Use it to help you plan your writing.

Introduction:		
Destination 1	Destination 2	Destination 3
Reason 1	Reason 1	Reason 1
Reason 2	Reason 2	Reason 2
Reason 3	Reason 3	Reason 3
Conclusion:		

Answers

Where Am I? answers, p. 48-49:

1. Lincoln Park Zoo, 2. Buckingham Fountain, 3. Water Tower, 4. Hyde Park, 5. Millennium Park, 6. Wrigley Field

Comprehension question answers, p. 53:

p. 6-7

The University of Chicago is located in Hyde Park.

Frank Lloyd Wright was a famous American architect from Chicago.

p. 8-9

The massive Museum of Science and Industry may have so many interactive exhibits because they are fun and engaging and help promote an understanding of science.

p. 10-11

The Field Museum is one of the world's largest natural history museums.

Sue is the largest nearly complete skeleton of a *Tyrannosaurus rex* ever discovered.

p. 12-13

Visitors can see a wide variety of aquatic creatures from around the world at the John G. Shedd Aquarium including lake sturgeons, turtles, coral reef fish, beluga whales, and otters.

p. 14-15

At Adler Planetarium, visitors can learn about outer space, see pictures of stars and constellations, check out the Gemini 12 spacecraft, and even look at the sun through the Doane Observatory telescope.

p. 16-17

Each of the four seahorses on Buckingham Fountain represent one of the four states touching Lake Michigan: Illinois, Indiana, Michigan, and Wisconsin.

p. 18-19

The Art Institute of Chicago is located in the Loop, the heart of downtown.

p. 20-21

Answers may vary.

p. 22-23

The Ferris wheel was invented in Chicago by George W. Ferris for the 1893 Columbian Exposition.

p. 24-25

After the Great Chicago Fire of 1871, the city needed to be rebuilt. Instead of using wood, steel was used. Rather than building out, architects built up. Eventually, the skyscraper was invented in Chicago.

p. 26-27

The name Chicago came from a Native American word for wild onions as these plants grew naturally along the Chicago riverbank.

p. 28-29

Because the Water Tower was built out of limestone instead of wood, it survived the Great Chicago Fire while many surrounding buildings burned.

p. 30-31

Answers may vary.

p. 32-33

Chicago's Lakefront Trail is 18 miles (29 kilometers) long and stretches from south of the Museum of Science and Industry to way north, past Navy Pier.

p. 34-35

Answers may vary.

p. 36-37

Lincoln Park Zoo opened in 1868 and was named after Abraham Lincoln, who lived most of his life in Illinois before becoming president.

p. 38-39

Many African Americans moved from the South to northern cities like Chicago as part of the Great Migration. They brought musical instruments and their personal histories, and paired them with the electric guitar to create the Chicago blues.

p. 40-41

Answers may vary.

p. 42-43

Wrigley Field was built in 1914 and has an iconic brick outfield wall covered in ivy. Its scoreboard is still changed by hand, rather than electronically, as a reminder of the field's history.

Glossary

architect, architecture *(AHR kuh tehkt, AHR kuh TEHK chur)* Architects are people who design buildings. Architecture is the art and science of designing buildings. It can also mean the style of buildings.

Chicagoan *(shih KAW goh uhn)* A person who lives in Chicago

engineer *(EHN juh NIHR)* A person who plans and builds engines, machines, roads, bridges, canals, forts, and similar things

Loop *(loop)* The heart of downtown Chicago. The city's elevated train tracks form a circuit, or loop, in the downtown area. The Loop is the neighborhood within and nearby this loop.

prairie *(PRAIR ee)* A region of flat or hilly land covered mostly by tall grasses

Index

www.ingramcontent.com/pod-product-compliance
Ingram Content Group UK Ltd.
Pitfield, Milton Keynes, MK11 3LW, UK
UKHW060104300726
14090UKWH00003B/376

* 9 7 8 0 7 1 6 6 5 3 2 7 1 *